I Like Biographies!

Read About
George
Washington

Aileen Weintraub

Enslow Publishers, Inc.

40 Industrial Road	PO Box 38
Box 398	Aldershot
Berkeley Heights, NJ 07922	Hants GU12 6BP
USA	UK

http://www.enslow.com

Words to Know

honor—To show respect to someone.

Presidents' Day—The third Monday in February, when we celebrate the birthdays of George Washington and Abraham Lincoln.

Revolutionary War—The war between England and America from 1775 to 1783. After the war, the United States of America was a separate country.

widow—A woman whose husband has died.

Library of Congress Cataloging-in-Publication Data

Weintraub, Aileen, 1973-
    Read about George Washington / Aileen Weintraub.
        p. cm. — (I like biographies!)
    Includes bibliographical references and index.
    ISBN 0-7660-2301-X
    1. Washington, George, 1732–1799—Juvenile literature. 2. Presidents—United States—Biography—Juvenile literature. I. Title. II. Series.
    E312.66.W445 2004
    973.4'1'092—dc22
        [B]
                                2004002312

Printed in the United States of America

10 9 8 7 6 5 4 3 2 1

To Our Readers: We have done our best to make sure all Internet Addresses in this book were active and appropriate when we went to press. However, the author and the publisher have no control over and assume no liability for the material available on those Internet sites or on links to other Web sites. Any comments or suggestions can be sent by e-mail to comments@enslow.com or to the address on the back cover.

Illustration Credits: All illustrations are from the Library of Congress, except as follows: Corel Corp., p. 21; Enslow Publishers, Inc., p. 13; National Archives, p. 15.

Cover Illustration: Enslow Publishers, Inc.

Contents

Chapter 1

Growing Up on a Farm

George Washington was a great hero in our country. He was born on February 22, 1732, in Virginia. He lived with his family on a farm.

As a boy, George did many things. He planted in his mother's garden. He played games with his older brother, Lawrence. He learned to ride a pony. When George got older, he even learned to dance!

George Washington was a great leader for America.

George grew up to be tall and strong. He became a leader among his friends. Everyone liked George because he was smart and brave.

George was very close to his older brother, Lawrence. So George moved into Lawrence's house. The house was called Mount Vernon.

Mount Vernon was a very large farm with many buildings.

Lawrence joined the army. Later, George joined the army, too. He was soon sent to fight the French. George was made a leader in the army. His soldiers did not have enough clothes to wear or food to eat, but they beat the French army.

George and his brave men fought the French in a war.

George went back to live in Virginia. He met a woman named Martha Custis. She was a widow with two children. George and Martha got married and lived at Mount Vernon. They grew wheat and raised horses on the farm.

George married Martha, a widow. She had a girl named Patsy and a boy named Jackie. George became their new father. See if you can find them in this painting.

11

George lived in a time before the United States was a country. England owned part of the land that is now the United States of America. But the people in America did not want England to tell them what to do. They wanted to be free.

This map shows what North America looked like when George was growing up. England and France owned most of the land, so Americans were not free.

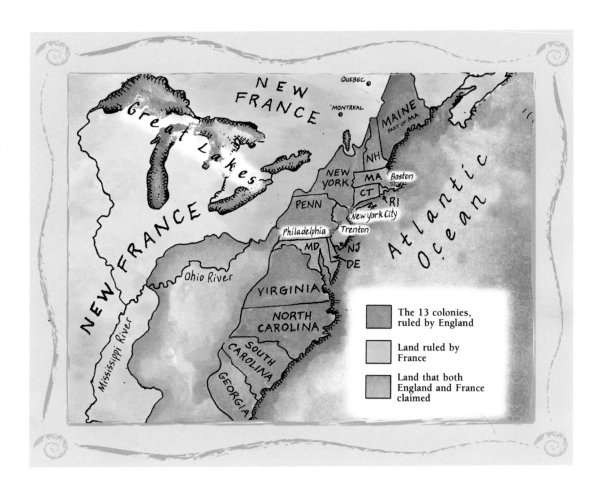

The 13 colonies, ruled by England

Land ruled by France

Land that both England and France claimed

Soon there was another war. This was called the Revolutionary War. It was a war to make America free from England.

George became the leader of the army. He and his men showed how brave they were. Many days, they were tired and cold. George told his men to never give up. They won the war against England.

During the Revolutionary War, George Washington and his army had to camp in the snow. But they did not give up.

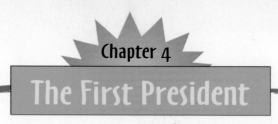

The people of the new country needed a leader. They picked George Washington. They thought he was the right man for the job. They knew George was brave and smart.

In 1789, George Washington became the first president of the United States. He was president for eight years.

The people of the United States chose Washington to lead the country. In this picture, he is promising to do his best to be a good president.

In 1797, George Washington went home to Mount Vernon in Virginia. He died on December 14, 1799. The people of the United States were sad. They called George Washington "the Father of his country."

George Washington became sick and died at Mount Vernon. He was sixty-seven years old. In this painting, Martha is holding his hand.

Now many places are named after George Washington. On Presidents' Day, we still honor all the hard work he did. He helped make the country we live in today.

Many places are named after George Washington, our first president. This is the Washington Monument in the city of Washington, D.C.

Timeline

1732—George Washington is born in Virginia on February 22.

1752—George joins the army.

1754—George fights the French.

1759—George marries Martha Custis and lives at Mount Vernon as a farmer.

1775—George is chosen to lead an army against England in the Revolutionary War.

1783—The war ends. The United States of America is free.

1789—George is elected president.

1799—George Washington dies at Mount Vernon on December 14.

Learn More

Books

Giblin, James Cross. *George Washington: A Picture Book Biography*. New York: Scholastic, 1992.

Jackson, Garnet. *George Washington: Our First President*. New York: Scholastic, 2000.

Mara, Wil. *George Washington*. New York: Children's Press, 2002.

Internet Addresses

George Washington: A National Treasure

<www.georgewashington.si.edu/kids/index.html>

Liberty's Kids: George Washington

<www.pbskids.org/libertyskids/arch_who_gwashington.html>

Index